STRENGTHENING AMERICA'S RESOURCE
&
REVITALIZING AMERICAN WORKFORCE LEADERSHIP

Strengthening America's Resource

STRENGTHENING AMERICA'S RESOURCE
&
REVITALIZING AMERICAN WORKFORCE LEADERSHIP

BRIAN SEXTON

authorHOUSE®

AuthorHouse™
1663 Liberty Drive
Bloomington, IN 47403
www.authorhouse.com
Phone: 1-800-839-8640

Published by AuthorHouse   02/23/2013

ISBN: 978-1-4817-1998-8 (sc)
ISBN: 978-1-4817-1997-1 (e)

Library of Congress Control Number: 2013903434

Table of Contents

I.

<u>Business Registration & Information</u>

Launch[21] Foundation, Inc. is incorporated in Illinois as a not-for-profit corporation with our corporate offices in Chicago, Illinois, and local offices in Kansas City, Missouri, Sarasota, Florida and Fresno, California. Outlined below is the pertinent information about our firm.

Primary Contact: Brian Sexton, Managing Director
Address: 25 E. Superior St. Ste. 4201, Chicago, IL 60611
Email: <u>bsexton@Launch21.org</u>

II.

Technical Factors

Launch[21] Foundation Background and Our Advantage

On Wednesday, January 12 2011, President Obama called on Americans to "expand our moral imaginations, to listen to each other more carefully, to sharpen our instincts for empathy, and remind ourselves of all the ways our hopes and dreams are bound together."

This is the purpose of our proposal.

According to a recent report issued by the San Francisco Federal Reserve, at least 200,000 additional jobs per month would be necessary to create a meaningful reduction in unemployment by 2013.[1]

Suppose the President were to issue an executive order requiring that one intern or trainee must be hired by a grantee or government contractor for each $500,000 of federal grants or contracts issued. For each intern/trainee, an annual wage of $15,000-$25,000 plus additional benefits of approximately $5,000 per year would be paid.

The total spending on government contracts and grants reached $1.1 trillion in 2010. Considering the $500,000 threshold for required participation in the program, this would correspond to an upper limit of approximately 2.2 million internships/traineeships created per year, or 180,000 internships per month. Given that certain military and health/social related grants and contracts (certain defense, health care, welfare, etc.) are included in the totals, we can assume that approximately one half or 1.1 million internships/traineeships could be realized. This would result in approximately 90,000 jobs per month, which would translate to an addition of 1.6 million jobs over 18-month duration of the program. The jobs created by this

---

[1]   Mary Daly. Bart Hoblin, Joyce Kwok. 2010. *"Labor Force Participation and the Future Path of Unemployment."* Federal Reserve Bank of San Francisco, Economic Letter, September 13, 2010

program would make a visible impact on unemployment, reducing it by 12 percent to a level of 7.7% by the end of 2012.

The results of this program are significant and have long term implications not only for unemployment numbers, but for workforce skill levels. In the long run, these changes could help lower US trade deficits by increasing national productivity.

The total 18 month cost of such a program would be less than $250 Billion and would be offset by the elimination of the need for unemployment compensation to employed interns/trainees. Actual 'productive work' and the development or enhancement of necessary skills would be the result instead of compensation for idle time.

Taking such meaningful and effective action to help remedy the current employment crisis requires prompt and creative leadership on behalf of the President of the United States. A struggling economy paired with high unemployment and the imminent loss of unemployment benefits for up to two million individuals make this a perfect time to implement a new program that addresses unemployment in an innovative and productive way. If predicted results occur, such actions are bound to have the support of the American people. Funds are available to the President of the United States under the American Recovery and Reinvestment Act of 2009 (ARRA) to take such immediate and bold action, and we feel that action must be taken now.

In fact, we believe that the urgency of such action is worthy of putting it on a wartime footing—it appears to be a missing ingredient in ARRA efforts, and can be quickly addressed and implemented. Action that can create over 1,500,000 jobs through existing ARRA funds within the next 18 months after implementation is worthy of close examination
Hidden behind the unemployment numbers is the fact that the number of discouraged workers, those not looking for work because they believe none is available, climbed to 929,000 in November (year), the most since records began in 1994. [2] The net effect of factoring in these "discouraged" workers puts the nation's "underemployment rate" which includes part-time workers who'd prefer a full-time position and people who want work but have given up looking at close to 17%. The need for a remedy is clear.

The purpose of this letter is to address the critical problem of unemployment and to propose a significant contribution to stimulating the economy. This effort establishes an immediately effective paid internship program for contractors through Federal Business Opportunities to be implemented in February 2011 and to be fully functional by summer 2011. This internship program would target unemployed workers who need to gain new job skills and experience while earning income. Recipients of federal contracts in excess of $500,000 would be required to hire a number of interns

---

[2]   Bob Willis and Courtney Schlisserman. 2011 "Shrinking U.S. Labor Force Keeps Unemployment Rate From Rising" Jan. 9 (Bloomberg)

based on the size of the particular contract and would be reimbursed by the federal government for the interns' compensation and benefits. Internships would last from 6 to 12 months, and interns would be provided with authentic assessment by the contractors to give them leverage for future opportunities in the job market.

Some real and immediate progress toward a solution to the unemployment problem is necessary—not only because the national economy is in desperate need of such progress—but from a political perspective as well—. Government action during a time of crisis aimed at improving the conditions of the unemployed is not without precedent, as demonstrated by Franklin Delano Roosevelt in the creation of the CIVILIAN CONSERVATION CORPS INITIATIVE (CCCI) and the Works Progress Administration (WPA) during the Great Depression. These actions have been effective in addressing the needs of the unemployed. Such action can be taken immediately to achieve positive results in states with critically high unemployment rates.

Even when job benefits and administrative and insurance costs are added to those figures, the federal government will have potentially created 2 jobs for less than the cost of 1 currently created by the current recovery act (ARRA). Detailed costs will be outlined later in this proposal.

Such a program is within the power of President Obama to create and implement immediately. As pointed out by Ann O'Leary, executive director of the Berkeley Center on health, Economic & Family Security at the University of California, Berkeley, School of Law and a senior fellow with the Center for American Progress, there is well-established legal authority for much stronger Presidential action to promote good jobs through the use of Executive Powers.

This internship program, once implemented, would have many benefits to contractors, unemployed workers, the federal government, and the overall economic recovery, and would not compete with any other program established for an alternative purpose to create jobs for repairing infrastructure (e.g. a revised WPA program). The internship program creates meaningful jobs and also begins to forge a pathway toward a new career.

- Such a program would give credibility to the campaign program of CHANGE.
- Contractors would have access to low-cost workers who would be eager to learn new skills.
- Workers would increase their viability in the overall job market while earning wages.
- The federal and state governments would spend less on unemployment benefits while utilizing a more cost-effective way to re-educate workers whose job skills are obsolete.
- Tax revenue and consumer confidence would increase while unemployment would decrease.
- The impact on unemployment numbers would be immediate and positive.

- The economy would recover faster as more people return to the workforce with the new skills they have learned in the program and money to spend.
- New skills learned or practiced through actual work in such internship positions increase employee marketability and increase chances of subsequent employment elsewhere.

This internship program could enhance the programs currently being proposed to help speed up the economic recovery and especially help improve the lagging unemployment numbers. Given the unusual circumstances of this recession and the danger of long-term high unemployment, the need for innovative solutions is pressing. We believe this internship program will help boost several job sectors and immediately help speed up the economic recovery as well as having long-lasting effects.

Consistent with bi-partisan support to limit the growth and scale of government, the internship program, while accountable to the White House, would be administered by the not-for-profit company Launch 21 Foundation from the private sector and itself be a source of jobs. Details regarding the private sector administration of this program are outlined later in this proposal.

This proposal addresses the following issues:

1) The need for such a program;

2) The proposed internship program;

3) The benefits of the program;

4) The costs of the program, including wages and insurance;

5) Implementation of the program;

    a) Eligibility
    b) Nature of the internship work
    c) Assessment documentation
    d) Tracking
    e) Quality Assurance
    f) Competent and Immediately Available Administration

6) Implementation Plan and Timetable

7) Our team

The Need For Such A Program

An Unusual Recession

Several different factors have contributed to make the recession of 2008 the most severe since the Great Depression of the 1930s. The collapse of the residential real estate and housing markets caused U.S. homeowners to lose more than $5 trillion, or about 17%, in value[3], triggering the financial crisis on Wall Street, which in turn caused the loss of more than 10 million jobs in 2008 and 2009[4]. The loss of so many jobs presents a danger to long-term economic growth. Despite some gains from the American Recovery and Reinvestment Act of 2009, by 2012, the U.S. Economy will still be 5.1 million jobs short of 2007 employment levels[5].

The GDP remained flat for much of 2009 even though the economy continued to lose jobs. This trend defies an economic principle called Okun's law, which postulates that employment rates are intimately tied to increases and decreases in the GDP[6]. In a "normal" recession, a flat GDP should have meant slower job losses, which was not the case. One reason for this unexpected discrepancy is an increase in productivity because of new technology, which allowed employers to maintain or increase output with fewer workers[7].

Hardest hit in the unemployment numbers were blue collar workers, workers without college degrees, construction workers, younger workers under 30, males, and low-skilled service workers. This phenomenon is referred to by the Center for Labor Market Studies as the Blue Collar Depression[8]. Generally, a lack of appropriate skills has caused these workers to become almost unemployable in the current labor market. Indeed, 67% of all job losses across the economy have been blue collar jobs[9]. Three key industrial sectors that employed these kinds of workers experienced the greatest job losses in the recession: construction, manufacturing, and transportation/

---

[3] Dan Levy, *"US Homeowners Lost $5.9 trillion since 2006 Peak,"* Bloomberg, December 9, 2009, http://www.bloomberg.com/apps/news? pid=newsarchive&sid=aoD0J3e1Hdxk

[4] Timothy J. Bartik, "A Proposal for Early Impact, Persistent, and Cost-Effective Job Creation Policies," *Employment Research*, Upjohn Institute, January 2010, 1.

[5] Ibid. 2.

[6] Mary Daly et al, "Okin's Law and the Unemployment Surprise of 2009," *FRBSF Economic Letter 2010-07*, March 8, 2010, 1.

[7] Ibid.; also Lawrence F. Katz. "Long-Term Unemployment in the Great Recession," Testimony for the Joint Economic Committee, U.S. Congress, April 29, 2010, 5, http://www.economics.harvard.edu/faculty/katz/files/jec_testimony_katz_042910.pdf

[8] Andrew Sum, et als., "The Great Recession of 2008-2009 and the Accompanying Blue Collar Depression: They Can't Make It Here," Center for Labor Market Studies, Northeastern University, March 2010, 2.

[9] Ibid., 7.

warehousing[10]. These three sectors accounted for more than half of all job losses through February 2010[11], and the sectors least affected by the recession (educational/health services and professional/business services) are the least likely to employ these kinds of workers[12].

Crime

The labor market is undergoing a fundamental shift, as workers are finding fewer viable employment options. The only positive news is that crime rates have continued to decline.[13]This is an another unusual aspect of the current recession, especially given the number of young and uneducated workers who are without jobs, the demographic most likely to turn to criminal activity during past recessions. The danger, however, is that this trend could reverse itself if high unemployment rates continue in the long term, and crime could start going up for the first time in many years, especially among the hard-hit blue collar sector.

The Hidden Unemployed

Beginning in the early 1960s, the U.S. government stopped including what it calls "discouraged workers" in the official unemployment figures[14]. These workers are defined as those who have been unemployed for more than six months, no longer receive unemployment benefits, have stopped looking for jobs, or have accepted involuntary part-time jobs. Some may also include skilled workers who are reluctant to accept lower-paying jobs and are holding out for the same income they had before being laid off, what some analysts call "retrospective wait unemployment"[15]. Generally, the official unemployment figure is lower than the actual number of unemployed workers, sometimes significantly so. When "discouraged workers" are taken into account, the actual unemployment rate is closer to 17.3%[16], rather than the officially reported 9.0%.

---

[10] Ibid., 3.

[11] Ibid.

[12] Ibid. 4.

[13] Federal Bureau of Investigation, "Crime in the United States: Preliminary Annual Uniform Crime Report, January to December," May 24, 2010, http://www.fbi.gov/ucr/prelimsem2009/index.html

[14] Kevin P. Phillips, "Numbers racket: Why the economy is worse than we know," *Harper's Magazine*, May 2008.

[15] Lawrence F. Katz, 9.

[16] Bob Willis and Courtney Schlisserman. 2011 "Shrinking U.S. Labor Force Keeps Unemployment Rate From Rising" Jan. 9 (Bloomberg).

Effects of Longer Periods of Unemployment

The longer a worker is unemployed, the more his or her skills deteriorate and the harder it becomes to find employment. And the longer a worker is unemployed, the harsher the long-term economic damage to both the individual and the economy as a whole[17]. Another sign that this is a different kind of recession is the troubling trend of a continued rise in unemployment despite a rise in job openings, indicating that those out of work for more than six months are not qualified for the available jobs[18]. In past recessions in the 1970s and 1980s, business and industry would lay off workers in the short term and rehire them later. Now, those jobs are not coming back, meaning that workers are unemployed longer, sometimes permanently, compared to previous recessions[19].

Another contributing factor in continued long-term unemployment is that U.S. workers are less mobile than in previous recessions and are less likely to move geographically to where the jobs are[20]. This is clear evidence that the credit crisis is creating "a geographic lock-in effect"[21]. Homeowners are reluctant to move if it means selling their houses at a loss.

Polarization of Labor

Various trends over the past 20 years, including the rise of the information technology industry, requiring educated workers with specialized skills; the globalization of the world economy; and the general increase in low-end service industry jobs, which pay lower wages and require less skilled workers, have caused a polarization of the labor market. As a result of these factors, job growth occurs at the high and low ends of the market, but traditional middle-class jobs are disappearing, resulting in ever-increasing income gaps between skilled and unskilled workers[22].

Large numbers of workers in this polarized labor market are facing long-term unemployment and long-term earnings losses, which can create a domino effect in the economy as a whole as these workers drag down the recovery and continue to underperform in the immediate future. When more workers are employed full-time, the government will see more tax revenue, and the ballooning federal budget deficit will decrease, improving long-term economic recovery.

---

[17] Lawrence F. Katz. 3.

[18] Ibid. 4.

[19] Ibid. 5.

[20] Ibid.

[21] Ibid.

[22] Ibid. 6.

The Underperformance and High Cost of the Stimulus Package

The American Recovery and Reinvestment Act of 2009 (ARRA) was expected to create or save at least 3 million jobs by 2010[23]. To achieve a full economic recovery, the economy would need to create 10 million jobs by 2011[24]. According to the FRBSF in a letter dated September 13, 2010, 200,000 to 300,000 jobs would need to be created *per month* to bring the unemployment rate down to 8% by 2012.[25]

As of September 2010, the economy remained far short of such robust job growth. New initiatives are needed more than ever. In addition, fiscal stimulus policies like the ARRA are overly expensive, and do not provide enough targeted incentives to create more jobs. Under the 2009 stimulus package, the cost of creating 1 job per year is more than $100,000[26]. To reach the goal of full job recovery via fiscal stimulus would then require an even larger expense of $900 billion. Following such a high cost plan conflicts the goal to bring down the federal budget deficit[27].

Government Contractors

For decades, the federal government has been outsourcing many of its responsibilities and projects to independent contractors. The exact number of firms hired by the federal government is always in flux, but at any given time there are at least 100,000 active contracts[28]. According to government reports, contractors have used about $16 billion in stimulus funds since 2009 and created or saved 30,383 jobs[29]. **That amounts to $526,610 per job**, more than 5 times the cost of direct stimulus job creation. A more cost-effective solution is needed, and the federal government should better oversee taxpayer funds allocated to job creation.

---

[23] Christina Romer and Jared Bernstein, "The Job Impact of the American Recovery and Reinvestment Plan," Council of Economic Advisors, Office of the Vice President-Elect, January 9, 2009, 5, http://www.illinoisworknet.com/NR/rdonlyres/6A8FF039-BEA1-47DC-A509-A781D12 15B65/0/2BidenReportARRAJobImpact.pdf

[24] Timothy J. Bartik, "A Proposal for Early Impact, Persistent, and Cost-Effective Job Creation Policies," *Employment Research*, Upton Institute, January, 2010, 2.

[25] Joyce Kwok, et al., "Labor Force Participation ad the Future Path of Unemployment," Federal Reserve bank of San Francisco Economic Letter, September 13, 2010. http://www.frbsf.org/publications/economics/letter/2010/el2010-27.html

[26] Ibid.

[27] Ibid.

[28] http://www.gao.gov/

[29] Brad Heath, et al., "Reports: Federal contracts saved or created 30,383 jobs," *USA Today*, August 12, 2010, 2A, http://www.usatoday.com/printedition/news/20091016/a_stimulusjobs16_st.art.htm

However, the sheer number of federal contractors and the employment and training opportunities they represent cannot and should not be ignored. Government contractors present a unique opportunity to act as job creation engines when the economy needs a substantial increase in new jobs.

Infrastructure, Green Initiatives, and the Global Green New Deal

President Obama has begun an initiative to retrofit federal buildings to lower carbon emission standards, a policy change in tune with the global green initiative. This mandate could create thousands of construction jobs in the years to come. Also, President Obama has mandated the development of renewable energy resources, a plan that will require the development of whole new industries with new skill sets for workers. While these jobs alone are not enough to meet necessary employment goals, they present a unique opportunity to retrofit many sectors of the underemployed and unemployed workforce, including construction workers, truck drivers, and manufacturing workers, some of the sectors hardest hit by the recession[30]. Some of these workers will require training, others will not, but the initiative is expected to bring in more independent contractors. Originally unfunded when passed, the Green Jobs Act of 2007 will bring in additional funds for the initiative, up to $1 billion[31].

In addition to the green retrofitting initiative, President Obama has proposed a massive infrastructure rebuilding program to repair and replace thousands of miles of roads, rails, and bridges[32]. Initiatives and funding are being proposed, but they could be used more efficiently to create a more skilled and better-prepared workforce. Our proposal would call for just such an initiative: federally sponsored paid internships with federal contractors. All of the pieces are already in place.

---

[30] Jennifer Cleary, et al., "Preparing the Workforce for the Green Jobs Economy," Research Brief, John J. Heldrich Center for Workforce Development, February 2009, 2, http://www.cdorh.org/empleos%20verdes/Heldrich_Center_Green_Jobs_Brief.pdf

[31] Ibid. 4

[32] "President Obama kicks off campaign with infrastructure plan," Reuters, September 6, 2010, http://www.msnbc.msn.com/id/39023909/

III.

<u>The Proposed Internship Program</u>

To address any perceived challenges, An Executive Order should encourage, but not mandate, the use of interns on such government projects. Rather, agencies "may" on a project-by-project basis, require the use of interns by a contractor where use of interns will advance the Government's interest in achieving economy and efficiency in federal procurement, producing labor stability, and ensuring compliance with laws and regulations governing safety and health, equal employment opportunity, labor and employment standards, and other matters.

While economists forecast a slow recovery[33], many of the current stimulus plans are too expensive and inefficient to solve the employment gap[34]. It is important that the government focus more on job creation, but in a targeted, more cost-effective way. The Office of Management and Budget and the Congressional Budget Office have studied the costs of a program of tax credits, work sharing, and public service jobs that could create as many as 5 million jobs by 2011, with a gross price tag of $276 billion, or about $33,000 per job created[35].

Our proposal would add another weapon to that arsenal, a federally subsidized internship program that would compensate government contractors for hiring selected interns and retrain them to better meet the demands of an evolving labor market.

The word *intern* implies a low — or no-pay position for an inexperienced worker who is fresh out of college or high school. This proposal calls for fully paid internships, but the general principle would be the same: contractors would have to make the final call on whether a particular position should be filled by a paid intern.

The program would operate through a portal similar to the Federal Business Opportunity Web site, currently a portal for businesses and service providers to bid on federal contracts. Our proposal would utilize a similar site as a clearinghouse for unemployed workers to find paid internships in the fourth arm of government.

---

[33] William A. Strauss, et al., "Economy on cruise control in 2010 and 2011," FRBC Letter Number 277, August 2010, 1-2

[34] Bartik, 4.

[35] Ibid.

Increasing Small Business Contractors

Indeed, the Small Business Administration's Office of Advocacy pointed out as early as September 2006 the discrepancy in the amount of subcontracting funds small businesses receive: small businesses make up 99.7 percent of all employer firms but receive only 40 percent of subcontracting dollars from the federal government[36].

Most government contracts are worth more than $500,000, and we propose to make that figure the equal of at least one paid intern. The higher the contract bid, the more intern positions would be filled. For example, a firm that wins a $2 million contract would then be required to hire 3 or 4 paid interns, the government compensating the contractor accordingly.

Internships would last between 6 and 12 months, depending on the length of the contract. Contractors would be required to evaluate each intern's job performance, giving incentive for performance, and increasing worker productivity. Interns who perform an unacceptable job will be reassigned to other industries more appropriate to their talent levels.

In addition, the internship requirement could be waived for contracts involving military support overseas, or the mandated interns could be limited to domestic contracts or jobs. Such a restriction would lower the cost of insurance for the program.

Internships Are Cheaper than Traditional Re-Education

Traditionally, when workers need to learn new job skills, they return to school at either a four-year or two-year college. Many take out student loans or seek government subsidies. Many people stay in the workforce during this process, but often at reduced capacities. Our program is unique in that it offers a way to learn new skills on the job, which lessens the strain on cash-strapped student financial aid programs.

The program would draw from all sectors of the labor market, from construction workers and truck drivers without college degrees to trade skills workers to office support personnel to middle managers. Anyone out of work for 6 months or more and interested in learning new job skills would be eligible to apply.

For example, an unemployed construction worker could learn how to construct wind turbines through the paid internship program, a practical skill that could help

---

[36]   SBA Office of Advocacy, "The Government's Role in Aiding Small Business Federal Subcontracting Programs in the United States," Paper #281, September 2006, www.sba.gov/advo

him find a permanent position in the emerging renewable energy industry. He could even land a full-time position with the contracting firm that first hires him through the program.

Internships would be offered to those who have been unemployed the longest and moving down the list to those who have just been put on unemployment.

Market Forces Can Guide Wages

Interns could be paid market wages, as is the general policy of the President Obama Administration[37], and the program would still be more cost effective than direct stimulus spending. The "minimum wage" for interns must be higher than the benefits they might receive for participating in unemployment benefit programs in order to provide them with the necessary incentive to work rather than to stand idly by.

Not Without Precedent

Subsidized internship programs are not without precedent and have proved their effectiveness. Probably the single most successful program is the 30+ year old California WorkAbility program where over 100,000 students annually are subsidized in work based learning programs funded by the state. This program enables students with disabilities to gain work based skills at no cost to the employer and, with a large degree of success based on follow up survey data, enables them to either enter a post-secondary educational program after graduation or to enter the work force as a taxpayer.

The California Department of Education completed a two-year study in 1981 that provided substantive information concerning the status of vocational programs for students with disabilities. Results of the study indicated that these students were not being adequately prepared for the labor market.

WorkAbility was initiated in November 1981 as a pilot project to test the concept of work experience for youth with disabilities.

The mission of WorkAbility is to promote the involvement of key stakeholders including students, families, educators, employers and other agencies in planning and implementing an array of services that will culminate in successful student transition to employment, lifelong learning and quality of life.

---

[37] "A New Urban Agenda for America: Rebuild the Middle Class," The Partnership for Working Families, undated, 2, http://www.workingeastbay.org/downloads/A%20New%20Urban%20 Agenda%20for%20America.pdf

WorkAbility continues to successfully conduct interagency coordination of services, which began with a September 1982 Employment Development Department, State Department of Rehabilitation and California Department of Education (CDE) non-financial interagency agreement.

Through a designation as one of the ten best transition programs of its type in the United States, WorkAbility has received national recognition of its success in matching young adults who have disabilities with employers who need workers.
Though there is a difference between subsidizing the unemployed and an internship program, but the principle is the same: *Subsidized programs, properly constructed, WORK!*

IV.

<u>The Benefits of the Program</u>

Such a program would benefit contractors, unemployed workers, and local, state, and federal government in several ways.

Contractors

Generally, people who have been unemployed tend to be more enthusiastic and hard working when beginning a new job. Contractors would benefit from this injection of energy. In addition, they would have first rights to offer full-time positions to suitable interns, saving on the cost of recruiting new workers. Contractors will also give something back to society: a healthier and re-educated workforce.

Unemployed Workers

Unemployed workers would benefit by having an income, learning new and marketable job skills, building personal connections, and having an opportunity to apply for full-time positions at companies where they have worked as interns. Interns will have the following non-monetary, but significant benefits: being productive member of the community, a breadwinner for their family, having confidence to take a chance on a new opportunity, a feeling of self-worth, a better quality of life. In addition, interns will be able to update their resumes with new learned skills gained from this program—helping their marketability and productivity in the workforce.

Local and State Government

The benefits of this program to local and state government will be significant. High unemployment affects local governments more than the federal government because the unemployed contribute less to local economies and sales and property tax revenues. High unemployment also weakens the local housing market. When more workers find good employment, those problems diminish, and state and local budgets strengthen. In turn, strong revenues lessen the strain on public funding in other sectors, such as education, crime, state unemployment and human services.

Federal Government

This program, coupled with other targeted job-creation initiatives, will lower the unemployment rate and the costs of unemployment insurance. It will also help lower the cost of government-initiated job creation. A six-month paid internship could create a full-time job for as little as $20,000.

With more people back in the workforce, tax revenue and the GDP will rise, deficits will decline. The consumer sentiment will improve, as economic health returns to the country. This translates to the bottom line of strengthening our economy and national confidence.

The Costs of the Program

If, as cited above, the cost of creating one full-time job via direct federal stimulus spending is about $100,000, and more than 5 times that amount when contractors do the hiring and training, this proposed program could create 2 full-time jobs for the same amount of money.

Suppose the beginning salary of a new intern is $15,000-$25,000 per year, all else being equal. Under this proposed internship program, a firm winning a federal contract valued at $2 million would be required to hire 4 interns, each being paid by the contractor and the contractor passing through the costs as part of their bids on federal government contracts for the 6-12-month length of the internships. At the end of the 6-12-month period, 4 workers will have been retrained, their skills more in line with the demands of the current job market, for a cost of between $60,000 and $100,000.

In addition, health insurance as well as worker's compensation will be provided for each internship as part of the federal subsidy, ensuring that each intern has the appropriate health insurance for the duration of the internship program consistent with the provisions of the new health insurance laws and federal employment policies.

Even when job benefits and administrative and insurance costs are added to those figures, the federal government will have potentially created 2 jobs for less than the cost of 1 created by the ARRA.

The interns themselves have learned new job skills while earning wages and contributing to the economy. Those workers will not have to leave the labor market to attend college classes, but instead will be receiving practical, on-the-job training.

Given the need for a robust job creation program, the political and economic concerns of long-term unemployment and high budget deficits, and the high cost of direct job creation through stimulus programs, the lower cost and practical outcomes of this internship program must be given serious consideration.

V.

Implementation of the Program

To implement this internship program, several factors must be considered:

- Eligibility for internships,
- Nature of the internship work,
- Assessment documentation,
- Tracking,
- Quality Assurance, and
- Competent and Immediately Available Administration.

Eligibility

Job market research, cited above, shows that many of the hidden unemployed are older workers whose job skills are obsolete. Many are blue-collar workers, but many have college degrees, or at least some college. The unemployed come from all walks of life, which can be a plus for this program as contractors would be able to select from a wide-ranging pool of candidates.

In general, all individuals who are currently on unemployment or whose unemployment benefits have run out would be eligible for internships in this proposed program. As a sign of our times, many of the currently unemployed workers were working in obsolete industries.

Nature of the Internship Work

The operative words to describe the nature of the internship work are "substantive" and "meaningful." Internships must involve work that directly relates to beneficial skills and competencies.

Federal contractors cover a wide range of functions and offer a wide range of internship opportunities, from data entry and computer programming to skilled labor and service positions to middle management and personnel positions. So the nature of internship work is virtually unlimited.

The US Department of Labor has a large database of occupational information called "O*Net." (http://www.onetcenter.org/overview.html) The site itself describes it's purpose and content as follows:

"The O*NET program is the nation's primary source of occupational information. Central to the project is the O*NET database, containing information on hundreds of standardized and occupation-specific descriptors. The database, which is available to the public at no cost, is continually updated by surveying a broad range of workers from each occupation. Information from this database forms the heart of O*NET OnLine, an interactive application for exploring and searching occupations. The database also provides the basis for Career Exploration Tools, a set of valuable assessment instruments for workers and students looking to find or change careers."

"Every occupation requires a different mix of knowledge, skills, and abilities, and is performed using a variety of activities and tasks. These distinguishing characteristics of an occupation are described by the <u>O*NET Content Model</u> which defines the key features of an occupation as a standardized, measurable set of variables called "descriptors". This hierarchical model starts with six domains, describing the day-to-day aspects of the job and the qualifications and interests of the typical worker. The model expands to 277 descriptors collected by the O*NET program, with more collected by other federal agencies such as the <u>Bureau of Labor Statistics</u>."

As described on the O*Net Website, "The Content Model is the conceptual foundation of O*NET. The Content Model provides a framework that identifies the most important types of information about work and integrates them into a theoretically and empirically sound system."

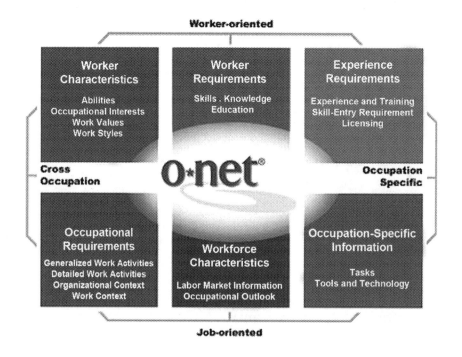

"The O*Net Content Model was developed using research on job and organizational analysis. It embodies a view that reflects the character of occupations (via job-oriented descriptors) and people (via worker-oriented descriptors). The Content Model also allows occupational information to be applied across jobs, sectors, or industries (cross-occupational descriptors) and within occupations (occupational-specific descriptors). These descriptors are organized into six major domains, which enable the user to focus on areas of information that specify the key attributes and characteristics of workers and occupations."

The internships in the program would be derived largely from O*Net and each internship defined in a format similar if not exactly like the O*Net structure. Additionally, each internship will be "matched" against either the "Critical Skills" or the SCANS Foundation Skills and Competencies (described below) to ensure that the internship has meaningful skill content and substance to provide the participating intern with a valuable experience which he/she can subsequently use.

Government's role would be to protect these interns from on-the-job hazards and make sure they are paid market wages and benefits during their internships.

Assessment Documentation and Authentic Assessment

Assessment of an intern's performance should be conducted, measured not only on how well an intern performs while doing assigned tasks, but on the skills and competencies that are associated with each of the tasks assigned. Without such an assessment element, some interns could underperform and not complete their retraining, undermining the purpose of the program.

Accordingly, a meaningful set of skills and competencies must be used and be consistent for all of the internships conducted in this program. Exactly what set of meaningful skills and competencies should be used is open to debate. Some skill sets focus on those skills and competencies needed in higher level jobs or are aimed at what is needed for any type of meaningful career—regardless of the industry or nature of the work. This set of skills, called the "Critical Skills," is taken from research conducted in the early 1990's and was published in Chief Executive Magazine as "Critical Skills and the CEO."

http://www.allbusiness.com/human-resources/employee-development/389800-1.html

The "Critical Skills"

Communications The ability to effectively transfer information from yourself to others or the ability to receive information from others through the processes of reading, writing, listening and speaking.

Analytical A two-part skill-1) the ability to gather and sort information relevant to a specific problem and ensure that the information to be used is accurate and applicable to the problem(s) being addressed; 2) the ability to derive from the facts a set of findings, conclusions and recommendations pertinent to the problem(s) being addressed.

Production The ability to take an idea and transform that idea into reality. This skill is essential from the simplest idea to the most complex and is often referred to as "making it happen."

Interpersonal The ability to demonstrate to others that you are a valued member of a team. This skill is not "making friends" or demonstrating social proficiencies, but actual and visible excellent performance on the job in the eyes of others.

Technology The ability to select the appropriate technology to solve a problem. This skill does not include the ability to design such technology—only to use and apply the technology toward providing useful solutions to problems.

Time Management The ability to set appropriate priorities on the job. An example would be recognizing that there are ten things that need to be done on a certain day, selecting the three or four most important things and doing them exceptionally well while managing to perform adequately on the others.

Continuing Education The ability to recognize that the world is changing and that technology advances rapidly render old skills obsolete. With such knowledge, the individual constantly strives to update his/her technological skills to meet the needs of a changing workplace.

The "Critical Skills" were developed from the examination of real world positions and were not the result of any survey. Accordingly, they represent reality and not simply the opinions of individuals surveyed. The skills cross industry lines and are timeless, i.e., they are just as relevant today as they were in the early 1990's. Additionally, they are "higher level skills" and not vocational tasks.

The "Critical Skills" and their application in the early 1990's led to the concept of "core competencies" which is in widespread use throughout industry. Core competency studies are frequently marketed by a variety of consulting firms and are recognized as essential for companies to use in developing recruiting, training, and assessment practices. However, such core competency studies tend to create an unnecessary level of complexity because consultants often consider that "more is better"

"Industry specific" and "functional" skills are different in that they focus on the skills needed for a specific job within a specific industry (i.e., the food industry, the auto manufacturing industry, etc.) or within a specific function (i.e., finance, marketing, human resources, etc.). These skills vary from job to job and, obviously, are important to be learned through any internship, but our position is that the primary focus should be on the industry indifferent "critical skills."

Another set of skills and competencies is a bit more general and focuses on lower level jobs. This set of skills is the enduring and timeless foundational skills and competencies developed by the Secretary's Commission on Achieving Necessary Skills (SCANS) in the early 1990s. SCANS formed the basis of the School-to-Work Act of 1992 (H.R. 5723). The "SCANS skills" were the result of a survey—not actual real world jobs—and outlined the necessary skills for the twenty first century and were based on a massive governmental and private sector effort to identify skills that cross industries and are relatively time insensitive.

The "SCANS Skills" consist of a three-part set of Foundation Skills and a five-part set of Competencies as follows:

The Three Part SCANS Foundation Skills

Basic having strong literacy and computational skills
Personal Responsibility showing maturity, commitment, and confidence
Thinking using creativity and higher-order reasoning to solve complex problems

The Five SCANS Competencies

Resources allocating money, time, staff, materials, and space
Interpersonal contributing to the team, clients, and customers through positive interaction
Technology understanding the productivity tools of the workplace
Systems improving the social, organizational, and technological systems in the workplace
Information acquiring, evaluating, and communicating data to team

Because SCANS was developed to assess high school students, internships would be assessed using a version of SCANS that can be modified and streamlined as needed. In other words, interns who have some college would not have to be assessed for writing and other basic skills all college students are expected to have learned by the first or second year of college. The individual circumstances of each intern can be considered and the appropriate SCANS model applied.

Simply testing an isolated skill or a retained fact does not effectively measure an individual's capabilities. To accurately evaluate what a person has learned, an assessment method must examine his or her collective abilities. Authentic assessment presents individuals with real-world challenges that require them to apply their relevant skills and knowledge. Thus, each relevant task that the individual performs *must* be "connected" to a relevant skill (SCANS); when performance of the task is assessed against meaningful criteria, the skills associated with the task may be assessed.

Of the two sets of skills—"Critical Skills" and "SCANS"—we recommend both "Critical Skills" and "SCANS" because of their simplicity and cross-industry characteristics as well as their new industry-level stature.

Authentic assessment accomplishes each of the following goals:

- Requires individuals to develop responses rather than select from predetermined options, or, in internship practices, the individual must perform; the individual must "demonstrate";
- Elicits higher order thinking in addition to basic skills;
- Directly evaluates holistic projects;
- Synthesizes with classroom or theoretical instruction;
- Uses samples of individual work (portfolios) collected over an extended time period;
- Stems from clear criteria made known to individuals—in this case, an adaptation of the "Critical Skills" or the SCANS foundation skills and competencies is used;
- Allows for the possibility of multiple human judgments, allowing an individual to have one or more supervisors who provide the assessment;
- Relates more closely to classroom or theoretical learning, meaning the individual can easily see the connection between what he or she is doing with the skills needed to be learned or mastered;
- Teaches individuals to evaluate their own work; and,
- Enables the creation of a "verified resume" to document skills.

"Fairness" does not exist when assessment is uniform, standardized, impersonal, and absolute. Rather, it exists when assessment is appropriate—in other words, when it's personalized, natural, and flexible; when it can be modified to pinpoint specific abilities and function at the relevant level of difficulty; and when it promotes a rapport between examiner and intern.

Authentic assessment is designed to be criterion-referenced rather than norm-referenced. Such evaluation identifies strengths and weaknesses, but does not compare or rank students.

Additionally, authentic assessment is often based on performance and/or demonstration. Individuals are asked to demonstrate their knowledge, skills, or competencies in whatever way they find appropriate. In this case, they demonstrate their knowledge, skills, or competencies through the tasks that they perform.

Using authentic assessment methods presents several challenges, including managing its time-intensive nature, ensuring validity, and minimizing evaluator bias. Therefore, consistent and meaningful assessment documents must be created for each specific internship and must be based on the actual position description for the internship outlining the purpose of the internship and the tasks to be performed.

This assessment tool needs to be developed and will be accomplished by one of our team members in this proposal, Dr. Arnold Packer, was the Executive Director of the SCANS Commission and one of the earliest voices in America arguing for the development of appropriate work-based learning skills in our educational system. He co-authored "Workforce 2000" in the 1980's which was an early alarm to America's competitiveness posed by the skills gap. In recent years Dr. Packer launched the Verified Resume process which teaches and assesses disadvantaged young adults in selected SCANS skills. Such a verified resume can be developed quickly to document the achievement of the "critical skills."

To further customize the "Critical Skills" or SCANS to the needs and skills of individual interns, and to reinforce the on-the-job retraining this program would mandate, a "Critical Skills" or SCANS certificate and verified resume will be granted to each successful intern who completes the program. This certificate will represent official documentation of that intern's successful retraining and could become a valuable asset for any new job the intern would find after completing the program.

Additional assessment needs to be conducted on the internship site (the contractor) as well. Specifically, the internship site must conform with the intent of the internship program—to provide a quality internship consisting of substantive duties as well as a meaningful connection between what the intern is actually doing with useful and transferrable skills. Such an assessment tool already exists. This is a quality management system in which specific internship site "expectations" are articulated and, for each of those expectations, specific "measures" set for measurement. These measures will be monitored by the administrative team through site visits, where applicable, with feedback provided by internship site management, through telephone surveys of intern supervisors, and the like. This methodology is consistent with that used by our team in the quality management system developed for the California Department of Developmental Services to measure the quality of care provided to consumers (developmentally disabled individuals) who were moved from large institutions and placed in service provider private homes for care in a smaller, but more effective, environment.

Tracking

Tracking of the internship program elements is essential and a system already exists that can easily accomplish this important task. This program will be very large in scope, requiring an enterprise-level system, and several specific elements will need to be tracked:

- Individual Interns
- Internship Sites
- Internship Content
- Assessment of Interns and Contractors

A specific database will be maintained for all individual interns. Information in this database will be confidential, but will not contain health information covered by HIPAA. Essentially, the data will be confined to personal information about the individual intern including contact data, social security number, appropriate insurance information, a personalized internship ID number and the internship site ID number to which the intern is assigned. This database will be "related" to the internship site database on a "one to one" basis through the internship site ID number and will be "related" to the internship content database through the internship position ID number.

A specific database will be maintained for all individual internship sites (contractors). Information in this database will be confidential and will be confined to specific contact information regarding the internship site. Included in such information will be relevant data concerning the contract under which the internship is covered, to include contact information for the internship site, the internship site ID number, internship content ID number(s) either specifically developed for that site or connected to a specific job description from O-Net.

A specific database will be maintained for all individual ASSESSMENT information. This database will contain the individual ID number as well as specific assessment ratings and commentary regarding the authentic assessment of the individual's performance in the internship experience. The database will be "related" to the individual intern database on a "one to many" basis through the individual ID number in order that the internship site might have the opportunity to conduct more than one assessment of the individual.

A specific database will be maintained for all internship site ASSESSMENT information. This database will contain the individual ID number as well as specific assessment ratings and commentary regarding the authentic assessment of the internship site's performance in the internship experience. The database will be "related" to the internship site database on a "one to many" basis through the internship site ID number to facilitate multiple assessments of the internship site's performance in the internship process through multiple sources against the established performance expectations and measures. Additionally this will allow the opportunity for multiple assessments of the internship site from any or all of these sources.

An existing software program, Coop2000®, designed to track such programs and incorporating skills and competencies already exists. For this internship program, we intend to license this software program and, with permission, provide the necessary modifications and simplifications to enable its use online. The system will enable administrators of the program to track individual interns, internship sites, internship positions, and all assessment documentation as well as the quality management system. The modification/simplification process will be accomplished through a subcontractor with broad experience with such systems, and should be ready for implementation on a trial basis within two months after the internship program is initiated.

System Architecture Design (Three-Tier Architecture):

The initial concepts for the modification and simplification of Coop2000® and its web-based application are as follows:

Web Servers:

Secure Web Servers utilizing (RAID 5) configuration stripes for both data and parity information across 5 parallel drives. Fault tolerance is maintained by ensuring that the parity information for any given block of data is placed on a drive separate from those used to store the data itself. The Operating System (OS) utilized will be no earlier than Windows 2003 and configured as an application / Domain Name System (DNS) server. The configuration of the Windows server will be both http and/ https for general and secure requests.

Team with IBM to deploy a virtualized, consolidated IBM BladeCenter solution that improves uptime and flexibility while simplifying the infrastructure. The system, running multiple operating systems concurrently, houses the organization's J.D. Edwards World enterprise suite along with a number of support applications.

Data-Base Servers:

Data-Base Servers. The Operating System will be no earlier than Windows 2003, and the SQL server will be no earlier than 2005. The Data-Base architecture will utilize industry standards of 3rd normal form, one : many relationship, many to many relations, and in some instances orphan tables. Server backup will be handled through third-party software and stored on encrypted external hard drives.

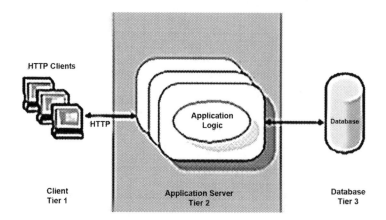

First tier: Responsibility for presentation and user interaction resides with the first-tier components. These client components enable the user to interact with the second-tier processes in a secure and intuitive manner. Clients do not access the third-tier services directly.

Second tier: The second-tier processes are commonly referred to as the application logic layer. These processes manage the business logic of the application, and are permitted access to the third-tier services. The application logic layer is where most of the processing work occurs. Multiple client components can access the second-tier processes simultaneously, so this application logic layer must manage its own transactions.

Third tier: The third-tier services are protected from direct access by the client components residing within a secure network. Interaction must occur through the second-tier processes.

Communication among tiers: All three tiers must communicate with each other. Open, standard protocols and exposed APIs simplify this communication. These clients run on any operating system, by speaking with the application logic layer. Databases in the third tier can be of any design, if the application layer can query and manipulate them. The key to this architecture is the application logic layer.

Application Architecture Design (.NET Three-Tier Architecture):

Presentation Layer (UI)
Presentation layer contains pages like. aspx or windows form where data is presented to the user or input is taken from the user.

Business Access Layer (BAL) or Business Logic Layer
BAL contains business logic, validations or calculations related with the data, if needed.

Data Access Layer (DAL)
DAL contains methods that helps business layer to connect the data and perform required action, might be returning data or manipulating data (insert, update, delete etc).

Quality Assurance

Consistent with all government procurement regulations and practices, quality assurance is mandatory and also essential from a political perspective. Our proposal meets the rigorous quality assurance standards and is built in to our system to report, in real time, all quality assurance issues, problems, and steps taken to improve practices or to correct any shortcomings. It is designed to comply with all regulations, be effective, and, because of the political sensitivity, completely transparent.

The only "products" provided by this program are the internships themselves—the selection of the interns, the substance of the work required under the terms of the internship, the authentic assessment of the interns, and the end-product provided to the intern in the form of a verified resume that will be useful to the intern in seeking and gaining subsequent employment after completion of the internship.

Accordingly, quality assurance inspection by the federal government must take place at the source where internships are coordinated as well as, at the federal government's convenience and discretion, at the site of the internships themselves. Additionally, we provide online monitoring of the quality management process through our internship coordination system.

Quality management has three major components: *quality control, quality assurance, and quality improvement*. We provide constant quality control of our activities through the selection and training of our team who, on a consistent basis, have a "quality attitude," and, in the sense of providing services to Interns, have *"been there, done that."* They know good quality service from poor quality services both from the perspectives of having been a recipient of such services as well as a provider. Hence, quality control is one of the fundamental parts of their work ethic. All have and continue to receive training for each of their positions as well as cross training in different departments which allows for a complete understanding of the challenges and the communication needed for quality control.

Quality Assurance focuses on real time measurement of the quality of services both at a macro level or at a micro level (providing remedies for problems identified by our QMS system). Quality assurance for the creation and development this internship program is built into three fundamental tiers:

1) A routine monthly progress reporting mechanism designed to demonstrate exactly where we are in the development and building process. This is our quality control on a "macro" level that enables us to show how we are performing against budget and plan.

2) An ongoing quality management system which will give our management up to date reports on the quality of services provided to our consumers. This is our quality assurance program on a "micro" scale. This system is not simply an "idea," but a proven system that was created to monitor the quality of service provided to individuals with severe developmental disabilities in the State of California. Its framework may easily be adapted to our services to participating interns.

3) Real time status reporting on the website showing immediate results of all quality management surveys among those who are participating as interns and among those contractors with whom the interns have been employed.

Quality improvement results from the combination of the "macro" and "micro" levels of quality control. Each plays a role in identifying problem areas. The macro level identifies problem areas in the implementation and management while the micro level identifies problem areas in the actual services provided to the intern. Together they form the backbone of our Quality Management System.

Competent and Immediately Available Administration

The ability to implement such a program exists now within the capability of the private sector. Mobilization of the required talent, while a significant task, could be expedited and in place within a couple of months and be ready to implement internships within a few selected 'battleground states' where such an effort is both needed and politically timely.

Participation by the private sector is entirely appropriate in such a national economic emergency. The talent is there, the systems either exist now or can be quickly modified, and the speed of implementation would be swift.

Administration of the program will be conducted by our team with the assistance of subcontracted talent. Essentially, this will be like running a very large educational internship program—but on a massive scale, and modified where needed to better assess the retraining of each intern.

As mentioned earlier in this proposal, time is of the essence and implementation will take place in a phased process with emphasis and initial implementation occurring in the key battleground states. Implementation steps will take place simultaneously and timed for completion in order that implementation in the battleground states can occur at the soonest possible time.

Implementation steps will include but not be limited to the following:

Initial Planning Meeting

- Establishment and agreement of administrative structure
- Establishment of quality management system criteria and accountability
- Establishment of internship qualifications and selection
- Establishment of target battleground states

Tracking and Reporting System Modification

- Selection and implementation of system modification process
- Select and retain system modification subcontractor
- Creation of the tracking and reporting system
- Pilot test of the tracking and reporting system
- Implementation of the tracking and reporting system in battleground states

Establishment of Quality Management System (QMS) Expectations and Measures

- Initiate QMS project to define expectations and measures for interns and subcontractors
- Create expectations and measures for interns and subcontractors
- Sign off on expectations and measures
- Implement expectations and measures into QMS System

Contractor Training

- Select subcontractor for contractor training
- Create contractor training materials
- Implement contractor training

Recruiting and Training of Sub Contracted Administrators

- Select subcontractor for system modification
- Select subcontractor for battleground state administration
- Select subcontractor for independent quality assurance auditing
- Select subcontractor for contractor training

Fully Implement Internship Program

- Select subcontractors for other states and regions, as appropriate
- Conduct subcontractor training

Implementation Plan and Timetable

Again, time is of the essence. If the program is started on or before March 1st, 2011, it would be able to be up and running for the battleground states by May 1, 2011 and fully operational for all states by July 31, 2011. For the purpose of this implementation plan and timetable, we make the assumption that sufficient funding will be available for full implementation by <u>July 31, 2011</u>.

VI.

<u>Methodology for Numerical Estimates</u>

In calculating the estimates the intent is to be conservative and not show unrealistic results. Rather, if the results are (statistically?) significant, the benefits of the program become more obvious.

Using "averages" is dangerous because, like in all things in life, the old "80/20 rule" applies. That is, 20% of the grants/contracts will account for 80% of the total value of the grants. In this case, we will be even MORE conservative and estimate that 20% of the grants account for 60% of the total value of the grants and contracts.

The methodology is to show the total number of UNEMPLOYED individuals, assign internships to contracts/grants on the basis of the $500,000 level for one internship, and then demonstrate how many of the unemployed can be given internships.

Example:

The civilian labor force in the US in February 2011

The unemployment rate fell by 0.4 percentage point to 9.0 percent in January, while nonfarm payroll employment changed little (+36,000)

"Many economists argued that the drop in the unemployment rate was real but it could easily rise if discouraged workers search for jobs again." The Labor Force Participation Rate fell to 64.2 per cent or the lowest level since March of 1984, or that the U-6 statistic which does not remove unemployed persons from the labor force merely for becoming discouraged moved from 16.6 per cent to 17.3 per cent. Furthermore, Canada—suffering the same weather over the same period—created 69,200 jobs on a population base of 35m compared with 36,000 US jobs on a population base of 310m.

The sharp decline in the unemployment rate from 9.4% to 9% and equally surprising anemic job growth-36,000 new jobs—left a lot of investors puzzled. How could the unemployment rate plummet so significantly while a such a trivial number of new jobs were created?

If we simply extrapolate those numbers, we get some nonsensical results. If adding 36,000 jobs to the 139 million jobs in the U.S. economy lowers the unemployment rate by 0.4 percentage points, then adding just 720,000 jobs should lower the unemployment rate by 8 points—from 9% to only 1%.

Yet the Bureau of Labor Statistics data shows that 812,000 jobs were added in the year from January 2010 to January 2011 (138,511,000 vs. 139,323,000). Based on the unemployment rate announced last week, we could expect that those 812,000 additional jobs would have lowered the unemployment rate to near-zero. But of course, we know they didn't.

HOUSEHOLD DATA Employment status
[Numbers in thousands]

	Seasonally adjusted[1]			
	Jan. 2010	Nov. 2010	Dec. 2010	Jan. 2011
TOTAL				
Civilian noninstitutional population.....	236,832	238,715	238,889	238,704
Civilian labor force...................	153,353	153,950	153,690	153,186
Participation rate.................	64.8	64.5	64.3	64.2
Employed........................	138,511	138,909	139,206	139,323
Employment-population ratio....	58.5	58.2	58.3	58.4
Unemployed......................	14,842	15,041	14,485	13,863
Unemployment rate.............	9.7	9.8	9.4	9.0
Not in labor force.................	83,479	84,765	85,199	85,518
Persons who currently want a job.	5,912	6,248	6,471	6,410

The basic reason why the numbers don't add up is that the BLS is constantly adjusting the variables of this basic equation:

Number of people in the workforce (civilian labor force)—number of people with jobs (employed) = number of unemployed people.

The BLS tracks the "civilian non-institutional population"—everyone not in the Armed Forces, school, prison, etc.—and the "civilian labor force." The category "not in labor force" includes everyone else, including "discouraged workers" who want a job but who have stopped seeking one.

This ongoing adjustment of who gets counted as part of the labor force leads statisticians to lower the unemployment rate—even though the number of employed people has barely ticked up.

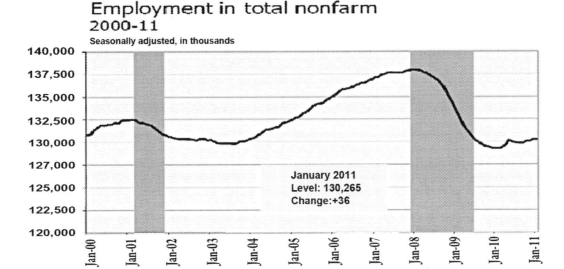

Employment in total nonfarm
2000-11
Seasonally adjusted, in thousands

January 2011
Level: 130,265
Change:+36

Using the BLS data, we can reconstruct what has happened over the past few years of recession and mild recovery.

The U.S. gains about 2 million new residents every year from births and legal immigration. For instance, the civilian non-institutional population rose from 236.5 million in October 2009 to 238.5 million in October 2010.

HOUSEHOLD DATA
Summary table A. Household data, seasonally adjusted
[Numbers in thousands]

Category	Oct. 2009	Aug. 2010	Sept. 2010	Oct. 2010	Change from: Sept. 2010-Oct. 2010
Employment status					
Civilian noninstitutional population..	236,550	238,099	238,322	238,530	208
Civilian labor force.................	153,854	154,110	154,158	153,904	-254
Participation rate.................	65.0	64.7	64.7	64.5	-0.2
Employed........................	138,242	139,250	139,391	139,061	-330
Employment-population ratio	58.4	58.5	58.5	58.3	-0.2
Unemployed......................	15,612	14,860	14,767	14,843	76
Unemployment rate..........	10.1	9.6	9.6	9.6	0.0
Not in labor force.................	82,696	83,989	84,164	84,626	462

Given this substantial increase in population every year, we might reasonably expect the civilian labor force to expand proportionally, as students graduate and new immigrants enter the workforce.

Yet according to the BLS, the civilian labor force was 153.8 million in January 2008 and 153.2 million in January 2011-a decline of 600,000 while the population increased by some 6 million. And the not-in-labor-force category expanded by 2 million from January 2010 to January 2011, from 83.4 million to 85.5 million.

When unemployed people stop looking for jobs at their local unemployment office, the government no longer counts them as unemployed. That's how the number of unemployed can drop from 15 million in November 2010 to 13.8 million in January 2011, a decline of 1.2 million, even though the economy created only about 400,000 jobs in those three months.

Over a longer time period, the not-in-labor-force group rose from 78.8 million in January 2008 to 85.5 million in January 2011-an increase of almost 7 million.

How do you drop the unemployment rate? Simple: remove 7 million people from the labor force.

The Real Unemployment Level Is . . .

If the labor force reflected the growth in population, then we might expect it to have increased by almost 2 million people a year. Rather than decline by 600,000 over three years, the labor force should have increased by 6 million to about 159 million.

If we take the number of unemployed as roughly 15 million (the BLS number from November 2010) and the true labor force as 160 million (out of an estimated total population of 310 million), then the true unemployment rate would be about 9.4%-right where it was before the recent adjustment to 9%.

Job Growth Is Still Weak

For context, let's look at some other employment numbers. According to the ADP National Employment Report in late December, the economy lost about 9 million private sector jobs during the recession—about 7.75% of all private—sector jobs.

According to the BLS, the U.S. had 138.2 million jobs in October 2009, a few months after the official end of the recession. Sixteen months later, the country had 139.3 million jobs—a gain of 1.1 million. That's a growth rate of about 880,000 new jobs a year. While that's certainly encouraging, this rate of job growth lags far behind those of previous post-recession recoveries as this chart depicts.

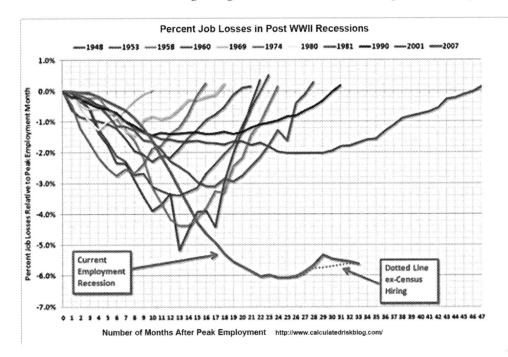

Bottom line: The numbers that matter in the U.S. economy are the total number of jobs and the number of jobs created, not the constantly massaged unemployment rate and not-in-labor-force numbers.

The total civilian labor force in January 2011 is 153,186.[38] The total number of civilian labor force unemployed in January 2011 is 13,900,000.[39]

The total unemployment rate in the civilian labor force in January 2011 is 9.0%.[40] Or (13,900/153,186 = 9.07% The total number of the civilian labor force that wants jobs is 8,400,000.[41]

The target population for an internship program is the civilian labor force that want jobs or 8,400,000 workers. While this is the target population, the calculations of the impact of the internship program should be made on the total number of unemployed workers, or 13,900,000.

Unemployment in Battleground States

The battleground states are:
Ohio

---

[38]   Source: Bureau of Labor Statistics. http://www.bls.gov/news.release/empsit.a.htm

[39]   Source: Bureau of Labor Statistic http://www.bls.gov/news.release/pdf/empsit.pdf

[40]   Source: Bureau of Labor Statistics http://www.bls.gov/news.release/empsit.t01.htm

[41]   Source: Bureau of Labor Statistics http://www.bls.gov/news.release/empsit.t01.htm

Michigan
Pennsylvania
Florida
Virginia
California

Ohio

Civilian Labor Force—Number of persons, in thousands, seasonally adjusted.	5,906,500
Employment—Number of persons, in thousands, seasonally adjusted.	5,339,900
Unemployment—Number of persons, in thousands, seasonally adjusted.	566,600
Unemployment Rate—In percent, seasonally adjusted.	9.6%

Michigan

Civilian Labor Force—Number of persons, in thousands, seasonally adjusted.	4,763,100
Employment—Number of persons, in thousands, seasonally adjusted.	4,207,800
Unemployment—Number of persons, in thousands, seasonally adjusted.	553,300
Unemployment Rate—In percent, seasonally adjusted.	11.7%

Pennsylvania

Civilian Labor Force—Number of persons, in thousands, seasonally adjusted.	6,357,700
Employment—Number of persons, in thousands, seasonally adjusted.	5,819,400
Unemployment—Number of persons, in thousands, seasonally adjusted.	538,300
Unemployment Rate—In percent, seasonally adjusted.	8.5%

Florida

Civilian Labor Force—Number of persons, in thousands, seasonally adjusted.	9,245,400
Employment—Number of persons, in thousands, seasonally adjusted.	8,137,100
Unemployment—Number of persons, in thousands, seasonally adjusted.	1,108,300
Unemployment Rate—In percent, seasonally adjusted.	12.0%

Virginia

Civilian Labor Force—Number of persons, in thousands, seasonally adjusted.	4,182,000
Employment—Number of persons, in thousands, seasonally adjusted.	3,903,400
Unemployment—Number of persons, in thousands, seasonally adjusted.	278,600
Unemployment Rate—In percent, seasonally adjusted.	6.7%

California

Civilian Labor Force—Number of persons, in thousands, seasonally adjusted.	18,214,800
Employment—Number of persons, in thousands, seasonally adjusted.	15,945,600
Unemployment—Number of persons, in thousands, seasonally adjusted.	2,269,300
Unemployment Rate—In percent, seasonally adjusted.	12.5%

Chicago Metropolitan Area
(For Information Only—Not Included in Battleground States)

Civilian Labor Force—Number of persons, in thousands, seasonally adjusted.	4,094,700

Employment—Number of persons, in thousands, seasonally adjusted.	3,742,400
Unemployment—Number of persons, in thousands, seasonally adjusted.	352,400
Unemployment Rate—In percent, seasonally adjusted.	8.6%

Battleground State Summary

Civilian Labor Force—Number of persons, in thousands, seasonally adjusted.	48,669,500
Employment—Number of persons, in thousands, seasonally adjusted.	43,353,200
Unemployment—Number of persons, in thousands, seasonally adjusted.	5,314,400
Unemployment Rate—In percent, seasonally adjusted.	10.9%

Battleground States as a Percentage of Total Labor Force:

Civilian Labor Force—Number of persons, in thousands, seasonally adjusted.	28.6%
Employment—Number of persons, in thousands, seasonally adjusted.	32%
Unemployment—Number of persons, in thousands, seasonally adjusted.	38.2%

The national unemployment rate is 9.0% in January 2011 (seasonally adjusted). Six states, Ohio, Michigan, Pennsylvania, Florida, Virginia and California comprise 28.6% of the total civilian labor force and 38.2% of the unemployed persons. The total unemployed in these six states is 5,314,400.

The main point here is to show that an initial focus on a few states can reach a large percentage of the unemployed more quickly.

VII.

<u>Government Grants and Contracts</u>

<u>Number of New Internships in Battleground States:</u>

The data below is a rough estimate of the number of new internships that our proposal would develop. This program will reach the critical mass that would allow every unemployed American the chance of learning new beneficial skills that will pave the way for them to enter into new careers.

State	Total $$ Contracts & Grants > $500K	Number of Grants & Contracts > $500K	Number of Potential Internships by State	Number of Potential Internships
CA	$101,057,659,976.56	14,400	7,017,893	7,017,893
FL	$35,922,082,409.00	5,543	6,480,621	13,498,514
MI	$24,919,495,038.40	3,018	8,256,957	21,755,471
OH	$19,836,351,099.27	3,503	5,662,675	27,418,146
PA	$36,075,523,077.95	4,786	7,537,719	34,955,865
VA	$52,789,409,609.79	16,110	3,276,810	38,232,675

We estimate this program will be a positive influence on the US job market by giving American workers additional training and skills, while reinforcing new roles and responsibilities.

At the end of each internship period, workers will be asked to submit a written manual detailing their job, roles and responsibilities. In addition, we will ask workers to make recommendations for better or more efficient ways of completing their job. This way, we can start distributing that education to the next wave of new interns. Thereby each new class of interns will learn and integrate "best practices" and be one step closer to full-time employment in the private sector.

VIII.

<u>Author's Approach and Capability Factor</u>

The mission of Launch[21] is to focus on skills development, training and internship placement of the current unemployed. The creation and development of Launch[21] organization has proven demonstrated abilities in the following areas:

- *Creating and managing startup ventures;*
- *Innovating and implementing new services such as online coordinating systems, skill assessment techniques, educational and skill development programs, and quality management and accountability practices;*
- *Serving the needs of the U.S. Government and Veterans looking to start businesses;*
- *Building, testing, and implementing services which are scalable to a national level.*

After performing a competitive analysis of the interested vendors list, Launch[21] stands alone at the top in terms of proven capabilities/track record and potential for delivering the highest possible quality that can be built, tested, and scaled upward toward providing service at a national level. That is our goal, and we intend to prove it through our performance.

Together we can achieve the goal of giving a job to every American worker.

Printed in the United States
By Bookmasters